May I Quote You, General Lee?

MAY I QUOTE YOU, GENERAL LEE?

*Observations and Utterances of the
South's Great Generals*

Randall Bedwell

CUMBERLAND HOUSE

PUBLISHING INC.

PUBLISHED BY
CUMBERLAND HOUSE PUBLISHING, INC.
431 Harding Industrial Drive
Nashville, Tennessee 37211
www.cumberlandhouse.com

May I Quote You . . . ?® is a Registered Trademark of Guild Bindery Press, Inc.

Some quotations have been edited for clarity and brevity.

Typography by The BookSetters Co.

Cover design by Gore Studio, Inc., Nashville, Tennessee.

Library of Congress Cataloging-in-Publication Data.

May I quote you, General Lee? : observations and utterances of the South's great generals / [compiled by] Randall Bedwell.
    p.   cm. — (May I quote you, General? series)
    ISBN 1-888952-34-2 (pbk. : alk. paper)
    1. Lee, Robert (Robert Edward), 1807–1870—Quotations. 2. United States—History—Civil War, 1861–1865—Quotations, maxims, etc. 3. Quotations, American. I. Bedwell, Randall J. II. Series.
E467.1.L4M46 1997
973.7'3'092—dc21   96-51927
                                                                            CIP

Printed in the United States of America

5 6 7 8 9 10 — 12 11 10 09 08

To my grandmother,
Rebecca Hartsfield Claxton

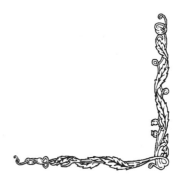

Table of Contents

Introduction ix

Chapter One
    Hard Choices 1

Chapter Two
    Fighting Words 13

Chapter Three
    Strategy and Tactics 21

Chapter Four
    Leaders of Men 31

Chapter Five
    Among Their Peers 49

Chapter Six
    Faith and Doubt 57

Chapter Seven
    Aftermath 67

Chapter Eight
    Last Tattoo 75

Introduction

Perhaps it is the perennial appeal of the underdog that enables these gray ghosts to maintain their hold on our imaginations. While they defended their way of life with conviction (but not without reluctance), in many of these statements they reveal themselves to be mere overwhelmed individuals, and understandably so. All their actions take place in a climate of national desperation unequalled at any other time in American history save for the Revolution. In 1861, the future Confederate commanders had every reason to believe that they would be hanged should secession fail. Lives, fortunes, sacred honor: Those were the terms in which the South's wartime leaders pledged their sacrifice.

Randall J. Bedwell
Cordova, Tennessee
October 1, 1995

General Robert E. Lee

CHAPTER ONE

Hard Choices

During the bleak interlude between Lincoln's election and the eventual commencement of hostilities, almost every future Confederate commander left some written account of his arduous decision to forsake the Union. Reneging on an oath was a grave matter, and early in their careers most of these fighting men had pledged their lives to defend the Union and the Constitution that binds it. Conspicuously absent from their remarks is any enthusiasm for a military solution to the secession crisis. With solemn tones they delineate their reasons: duty, honor, principle.

★ ★ ★

1

My loyalty to Virginia ought to take precedence over that which is due to the federal government. If Virginia stands by the old Union, so will I. But, if she secedes, then I will still follow my native state with my sword, and need be with my life.

—*Robert E. Lee to Charles Anderson,*
February 1861

I owe all that I
am to the government
of the United States. It has
educated and clothed me with
honor. To leave the service is a hard
necessity, but I must go. Though I am
resigning my position, I trust I may
never draw my sword against
the old flag.

—*Joseph E. Johnston*

There is no sacrifice I am not ready to make for the preservation of the Union save that of honor.

—Robert E. Lee to his wife, Mary Custis Lee, January 1861

Our present political system has been achieved in a manner unprecedented in the history of nations. . . . It illustrates the American idea that governments rest on the consent of the governed, and that it is the right of the people to alter or abolish them at will whenever they become destructive of the ends for which they were established. Obstacles may retard, but they can not long prevent the progress of a movement sanctified by its justice and sustained by a virtuous people.

—President Jefferson Davis's inaugural address, Montgomery, Alabama, February 1861

I take great
pride in my country, her
prosperity and institutions,
and would defend any state if
her rights were invaded. But I can
anticipate no greater calamity for the
country than the dissolution of the Union.
It would be an accumulation of all the
evils we complain of, and I am
willing to sacrifice every-
thing but honor for its
preservation.

—*Robert E. Lee*

It seems like fate that Texas has made me a rebel twice.

—*Albert Sidney Johnston, referring to his participation in the War for Texas Independence from Mexico*

People who are anxious to bring on war don't know what they are bargaining for; they don't see all the horrors that must accompany such an event.

—*Stonewall Jackson*

I have broken all ties that bind me to the [U.S.] Army, not suddenly, impulsively, but conscientiously and after due deliberation. I sacrifice more to my principles than any other officer in the Army can do. I would rather carry a musket in the cause of the South than be commander-in-chief under Mr. Lincoln.

—*Edmund Kirby Smith*

The line of duty
is clear. Each one to
follow his own state if
his state goes to war; if
not, he may remain and
help on the work
of reunion.

—*Matthew Fontaine Maury*

I must side either with or against my section or country. I cannot raise my hand against my birthplace, my home, my children. I should like, above all things, that our difficulties might be peaceably arranged. . . . Whatever may be the result of the contest, I foresee that the country will have to pass through a terrible ordeal, a necessary expiation perhaps for our national sins.

—*Robert E. Lee, excerpt from a letter to a Northern girl who had requested his photograph*

As we are now
engaged in this contest,
all my wishes, all my desires
and all the energies of my hand
and heart will be given to the cause
of my state. Whether we have the
right of secession or revolution, I
want to see my state
triumphant.

—Jubal Early

James Longstreet

CHAPTER TWO

Fighting Words

With the fate of nations hanging in the balance, little wonder that things said under the stress of battle often seem masterpieces of understatement. Though hostile circumstances dictated brevity, the power of such statements lies in their pith, and the history of warfare is replete with examples of such stirring words. The heightened adrenalin-induced awareness brought about by combat—what Winston Churchill called the "exhilaration" of being shot at and missed—loosens poetry in men. What they say sometimes means the difference between victory and defeat.

There is Jackson standing like a stone wall. Let us determine to die here, and we will conquer.

—General Barnard E. Bee describing Thomas J.
"Stonewall" Jackson's brigade at
First Bull Run, 1861

You have your bayonets!

—Thomas C. Hindman's response to a subordinate who
advised against mounting a charge due to a
lack of ammunition, Shiloh, 1862

Major, send a shell first over their heads and let them get in their holes before you open with all your guns.

—John Bell Hood, advancing up the Rappahannock, 1863

We shall attack at daylight tomorrow. I would fight them if they were a million.

—Albert Sidney Johnston, Shiloh, 1862

Form platoons! Draw saber! Charge!

—J.E.B. Stuart's standard cavalry order

I did not come here for the purpose of surrendering my command.

—*Nathan Bedford Forrest, Fort Donelson, 1862*

Tonight we will water our horses in the Tennessee River.

—*Albert Sidney Johnston, Shiloh, 1862*

General Lee: How many men will you take?

General Jackson: My whole corps.

General Lee: Well, go on.

—*Last words exchanged between Robert E. Lee and Stonewall Jackson, Chancellorsville, 1863. It was decided there to risk dividing the Confederate force in a bold flanking march to turn Hooker's right.*

Now, gentlemen, let tomorrow be their Waterloo!

—P. G. T. Beauregard, First Bull Run, 1861

Alabama soldiers, all I ask of you is to keep up with the Texans!

—Robert E. Lee, preparing to advance,
the Wilderness, 1864

If you surrender, you shall be treated as prisoners of war, but if I have to storm your works, you may expect no quarter.

—Nathan Bedford Forrest

Don't get scared, now that we have got them whipped.

—James Longstreet to D. H. Hill, Malvern Hill, 1862

Up, men, and to your posts! Don't forget today you are from Old Virginia.

—General George Pickett, Gettysburg, 1863

Colonel Carroll: General, a heavy line of infantry is in our rear. We're between two lines of battle. What'll we do?

General Forrest: Charge both ways!

—Brice's Cross Roads

It is well
that war is so
terrible, else men
would learn to love
it too much.

—*Robert E. Lee,*
Fredericksburg, 1862

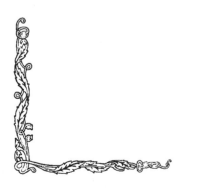

Nathan Bedford Forrest

CHAPTER THREE

Strategy and Tactics

Military scholars point to the War Between the States as the first truly modern war. Their assessment is due in part to the inspired tactical innovations made by Southern commanders to compensate for their lack of troop strength and reliable arms. While the maxims of warfare that follow may sound like common sense, in the thick of battle, they proved to be words of uncommon genius.

★ ★ ★

An invasion of the enemy's country breaks up all his preconceived plans of invasion.

—*Robert E. Lee*

Once you get them running, you can stay on top of them, and that way a small force can defeat a large one every time.

—*Stonewall Jackson*

War means fighting, and fighting means killing.

—*Nathan Bedford Forrest*

If we can defeat
or drive the armies
of the enemy from the
field, we shall have peace.
All our efforts and energies
should be devoted to
that object.

—*Robert E. Lee to Jefferson Davis,*
July 6, 1864

Always mystify, mislead and surprise the enemy; and when you strike and overcome him, never let up in the pursuit. Never fight against heavy odds if you can hurl your own force on only a part of your enemy and crush it. A small army may thus destroy a large one, and repeated victory will make you invincible.

—*Stonewall Jackson*

We have an army far better adapted to attack than to defend. Let us fight at advantage before we are forced to fight at disadvantage.

—*J. E. B. Stuart, 1862*

There has always been a hazard in military movements, but we must decide between the positions of inaction and the risk of action.

—*Robert E. Lee*

It is important that conflict not be provoked until we are ready.

—*Robert E. Lee, 1861*

If we cannot be successful in defeating the enemy should he advance, a kind Providence may enable us to inflict a terrible wound and effect a safe retreat in the event of having to fall back.

—*Stonewall Jackson to Joseph E. Johnston, 1862*

The road to glory cannot be followed with much baggage.

—*Richard Stoddert "Dick" Ewell, 1862,*
on the necessity of small wagon trains

Apparent failure often proves a blessing.

—*Robert E. Lee*

Never stand and take a charge, . . . charge them too.

—*Nathan Bedford Forrest*

Shoot the brave officers, and the cowards will run away and take the men with them.

—*Stonewall Jackson to Dick Ewell*

It is easier to
defend a railroad by
massing troops at salient
and commanding points to
repress the attack of the enemy
and strike him if he advances,
than to extend the force
along the whole line.

—*Robert E. Lee*

Get there first with the most men.

—*Nathan Bedford Forrest*

It is sometimes better to wait until you are attacked.

—*Robert E. Lee*

Joseph E. Johnston

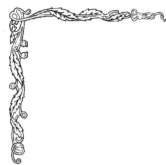
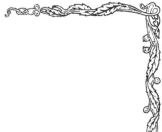

CHAPTER FOUR

Leaders of Men

Nothing could do more to improve a soldier's effectiveness than a few heartfelt words of praise and encouragement from his commanding officer. Ranging from martial oratory and edifying counsel to answering the army's critics, these statements encompass all aspects of the unique relationship between commanders and their troops, including what was perhaps the hardest to bear—the transition from war to peace via defeat.

★ ★ ★

There is only one attitude in which I never should be ashamed of your seeing my men, and that is when they are fighting.

—*Robert E. Lee, discounting the ragtag appearance of his troops to a British correspondent*

Your little army, derided for its want of arms, derided for its lack of all the essential material of war, has met the grand army of the enemy, routed it at every point, and now it flies, inglorious in retreat before our victorious columns. We have taught them a lesson in their invasion of the sacred soil of Virginia.

—*President Jefferson Davis, Manassas, Virginia, 1861*

Now, gentlemen, let us at once to bed, and see if tomorrow we cannot do something.

—Stonewall Jackson to his soldiers after a day of profitless marching

Keep steadily in the view of the great principles for which you contend. . . . The safety of your homes and the lives of all you hold dear depend upon your courage and exertions. Let each man resolve to be victorious, and that the right of self-government, liberty and peace shall find him a defender.

—Robert E. Lee's speech to his soldiers, September 9, 1861

I yield to no man in sympathy for the gallant men under my command; but I am obliged to sweat them tonight, that I may save their blood tomorrow.

—*Stonewall Jackson, 1862*

I need not tell
the brave survivors of
so many hard-fought battles
who have remained steadfast to
the last that I have consented to this
result from no distrust from them; but
feeling that valor and devotion could
accomplish nothing that could compensate for the loss that attended the con-
tinuance of the contest, I determined
to avoid the useless sacrifice of those
whose past services have endeared
them to their countrymen.

—From Lee's final letter to his men

I am sorry that the movements of our armies cannot keep pace with the expectations of the editors of the papers. I know they can arrange things satisfactory to themselves on paper. I wish they could do so in the field.

—*Robert E. Lee, 1861*

I will lead you. Follow me.

—*General Joseph E. Johnston*

The test of merit in my profession, with the people, is success. It is a hard rule, but I think it right.

—Albert Sidney Johnston, responding to public outcry against him after the loss of Forts Henry and Donelson, 1862

The soldiers know their duties better than the general officers do.

—Robert E. Lee

The army did all it could. I fear I required of it impossibilities.

—*Lee absolving the troops of responsibility for*
failure at Gettysburg, 1863

No matter what may be the ability of the officer, if he loses the confidence of his troops, disaster must sooner or later ensue.

—*Lee to Jefferson Davis, 1863*

I have never on
the field of battle sent
you where I was unwilling
to go myself, nor would I now
advise you to a course which I felt
myself unwilling to pursue. You have
been good soldiers. You can be good
citizens. Obey the laws, preserve
your honor, and the government
to which you have surrendered
can afford to be and will
be magnanimous.

—*Nathan Bedford Forrest*

I have done the best I could do for you.
Go home now, and if you make as good citizens as you have soldiers, you will do well,
and I shall always be proud of you.
Goodbye, and God bless you all.

—*Lee's last words to his troops at Appomattox, 1865*

I've got no respect for a young man who
won't join the colors.

—*Nathan Bedford Forrest*

This army stays here until the last wounded man is removed. Before I will leave them to the enemy, I will lose many more men.

—*Stonewall Jackson, Winchester, 1862*

They have stood it . . . nobly, but if it happens again, I shall join one of their camps and share their wants with them; for I will never allow them to suppose that I feast while they suffer.

—*P. G. T. Beauregard, upon learning that some of his regiments were without food, 1861*

Close up, men, close up; push on, push on.

—*Stonewall Jackson, his commonly used phrase*

Do your duty in all things. You cannot do more. You should never wish to do less.

—*Robert E. Lee*

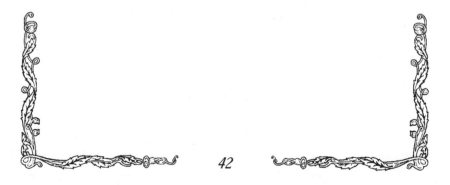

Civil war, such as
you have just passed through,
naturally engenders feelings of
animosity, hatred and revenge. It is
our duty to divest ourselves of all such
feelings, and, so far as it is in our power
to do so, to cultivate feelings toward
those with whom we have so long con-
tested, and heretofore so widely but
honestly differed. Whatever your re-
sponsibilities may be to government,
to society or to individuals,
meet them like men.

—Nathan Bedford Forrest,
farewell address to his men,
May 9, 1865

There is a true glory and a true honor: the glory of duty done—the honor of the integrity of principle.

—*Robert E. Lee, Appomattox, 1865*

I have been up to see the Congress, and they don't seem to be able to do anything except eat peanuts and chew tobacco while my army is starving.

—*Robert E. Lee, near the end of the war*

When a man makes a mistake, I call him to my tent, talk to him and use the authority of my position to make him do the right thing next time.

—Robert E. Lee

My experience through life has convinced me that, while moderation and temperance in all things is commendable and beneficial, abstinence from spirituous liquors is the best safeguard of morals and health.

—Robert E. Lee, 1869

Any man who is in favor of a further prosecution of this war is a fit subject for a lunatic asylum, and ought to be sent there immediately.

—*Nathan Bedford Forrest*

Never take counsel of your fears.

—*Stonewall Jackson*

Young gentleman, we have no printed rules. We have but one rule here, and it is that every student must be a gentleman.

—*Robert E. Lee, as president of Washington College*

We gain successes but after every fight there comes in to me an ominous paper marked "casualties," "killed" and "wounded." Sad words which carry anguish to so many hearts. And we have scarcely time to bury the dead as we push on in the same deadly strife.

—Wade Hampton, letter to his sister, 1864

Whatever happens, know this, that no men ever fought better than those who have stood by me.

—Robert E. Lee, Clover Hill, 1865

J. E. B. Stuart

CHAPTER FIVE

Among Their Peers

The effectiveness of the Confederate high command was impaired by numerous personality conflicts. However, at a time when a generation of commanders considered Napoleon to be the military ideal, the situation perhaps could have been worse. Lee's comportment, in fact, proved him to be anything but an egomaniac. Critics contend that he was polite and accommodating to stubborn, shortsighted subordinates, while lesser talents like Bragg and Beauregard could be unbelievably petty and recalcitrant. But if there was frustration, there was also glory, as exemplified by the rare coordination of purpose between Lee and Jackson, and Forrest's stunning successes despite his gains being underexploited by inept superiors.

General Longstreet, when once in a fight, was a most brilliant soldier; but he was the hardest man to move I had in my army.

—*Robert E. Lee*

I know not how to replace him.

—*Robert E. Lee at Stonewall Jackson's funeral*

If I had had Stonewall Jackson with me, so far as man can see, I should have won the battle of Gettysburg.

—*Robert E. Lee*

Such an executive officer the sun never shone on. I have but to show him my design, and I know that it can be done, it will be done. . . . Straight as the needle to the pole he advanced to the execution of my purpose.

—*Robert E. Lee on Stonewall Jackson*

I will be in my coffin before I will fight again under your command.

—Nathan Bedford Forrest to Joe Wheeler

Colonel Walker, did it ever occur to you that General Jackson is crazy?

—Dick Ewell

In advance, his trains were left far behind.
In retreat, he would fight for a wheelbarrow.

—*Dick Taylor on Stonewall Jackson*

The shot that struck me down is the very
best that has been fired for the Southern
cause yet. For I possess in no degree the confidence of our government, and now they
have in my place someone who does . . .
and who can accomplish what I never could
have done—the concentration of our armies
for the defense of the capital of the
Confederacy.

—*A wounded Joseph E. Johnston upon Robert E. Lee's
assumption of command of the Army of
Northern Virginia*

If you ever again try to interfere with me or cross my path, it will be at the peril of your life.

—*Nathan Bedford Forrest to Braxton Bragg*

A man I have never seen, sir. His name is Forrest.

—*Robert E. Lee's response when asked who was the*
greatest soldier under his command,
Appomattox, 1865

I do not mean to say that he is not competent, but from what I have seen of him I do not know that he is.

—*Robert E. Lee of his artillery chief,*
General W. N. Pendleton

The general is a little nervous this morning; he wishes me to attack; I do not wish to do so without Pickett. I never like to go into battle with one boot off.

—*James Longstreet on Robert E. Lee, Gettysburg, 1863*

A. P. Hill

CHAPTER SIX

Faith and Doubt

When Confederate commanders invoked the name of God, it was the Old Testament Jehovah they had in mind. Lee and Jackson, two men of unshakable faith, always attributed their success to Him. But they shouldered responsibility for the failures themselves. They alternated between the certainty of their simple Christian convictions and bleak moments of self-doubt.

At present, I am not concerned with results. God's will ought to be our aim, and I am quite contented that His designs should be accomplished and not mine.

—*Robert E. Lee, 1861*

Our God was my shield. His protecting care is an additional cause for gratitude.

—*Stonewall Jackson, Winchester, 1862*

I am truly grateful to the Giver of Victory for having blessed us in our terrible struggle. I pray He may continue.

—*Robert E. Lee to Stonewall Jackson, 1862*

So far as I can see, my course was a wise one; the best that I could do under the circumstances, though very distasteful to my feelings; and I hope and pray to Our Heavenly Father that I may never again be circumstanced as on that day.

—Stonewall Jackson after fighting a battle on Sunday, Winchester, 1862

How easily I could be rid of this, and be at rest. I have only to ride along the line and all will be over.

—Robert E. Lee on the morning of Appomattox, 1865

Sacrifices! Have I not made them? What is my life here but a daily sacrifice?

—Stonewall Jackson, in a resignation letter
that was never acted upon, 1862

Our enemies are pressing us everywhere. . . . I pray that the great God may aid us, and am endeavoring by every means in my power to bring out the troops and hasten them to their destination.

—Robert E. Lee, 1862

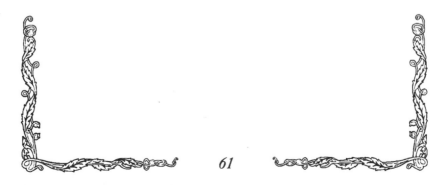

I tremble for my
country when I hear of
confidence expressed in me.
I know too well my weakness,
that our only hope is
in God.

—Robert E. Lee to his wife, 1862

If you desire to be more heavenly minded, think more of the things of heaven, and less of the things of earth.

—*Stonewall Jackson*

I can only say that I am nothing but a poor sinner, trusting in Christ alone for salvation.

—*Robert E. Lee*

I am too old to command this army. We should never have permitted [the enemy] to get away.

—*Robert E. Lee*

After it is all over, as stupid a fellow as I am can see the mistakes that were made. I notice, however, that my mistakes are never told me until it is too late.

—*Robert E. Lee to his officers after Gettysburg, 1863*

No, you greatly overestimate my capacity for usefulness. A better man will soon be sent to take my place.

—Stonewall Jackson, 1861

Colonel, when I lose my temper, don't let it make you angry.

—Robert E. Lee to his military secretary

Conscious of
my imperfections and
the little claim I have to be
classed among Christians, I know
the temptations and trials I shall have
to pass through. May God enable me
to perform my duty and not suffer
me to be tempted beyond
my strength.

—Robert E. Lee, 1861

Stonewall Jackson

CHAPTER SEVEN

Aftermath

Troubled by the ominous outlook of the region's imminent political fortunes, leading figures of the Southern cause adopted a message of reunion and reconciliation in the years following the war.

★ ★ ★

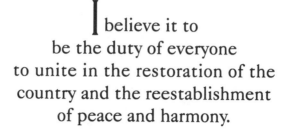

I believe it to
be the duty of everyone
to unite in the restoration of the
country and the reestablishment
of peace and harmony.

—*Robert E. Lee*

I believe I may say,
looking into my own heart,
and speaking as in the presence
of God, that I have never known
one moment of bitterness
or resentment.

—*Robert E. Lee, commenting on his feelings
toward the North after the war*

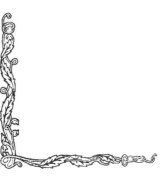

We must look to the rising generation for the restoration of the country.

—*Robert E. Lee to Governor John Letcher, August 1865*

I have fought against the people of the North because I believed they were seeking to wrest from the South its dearest right. But I have never cherished toward them bitter or vindictive feelings, and I have never seen the day when I did not pray for them.

—*Robert E. Lee*

The past is dead:
let it bury its dead, its hopes
and its aspirations; before you
lies the future—a future full
of golden promise.

—*Jefferson Davis*

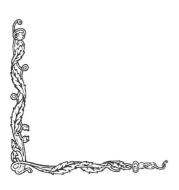

For an enemy so
relentless in the war for
our subjugation, we could not
be expected to mourn; yet, in view of
its political consequences, it could
not be regarded otherwise than
as a great misfortune for
the South.

—Jefferson Davis on the assassination of Lincoln

This news [of Lincoln's assassination] is the greatest possible calamity to the South.

—*Joseph E. Johnston to William T. Sherman*

This is not the fate to which I invited you when the future was rose-colored for us both; but I know you will bear it even better than myself, and that, of us two, I alone will ever look back reproachfully on my career.

—*Jefferson Davis to his wife from his prison cell at Fortress Monroe, 1865*

P. G. T. Beauregard

CHAPTER EIGHT

Last Tattoo

Their final words are a ready source of endless fascination. Some had the luxury of longer reflection, along with the obligation to eulogize those who died before them. Many met their end sooner on the battlefield.

⋆ ⋆ ⋆

Death, in its silent,
sure march is fast gathering those
whom I have longest loved, so that
when he shall knock at my door, I
will more willingly follow.

—*Robert E. Lee, 1869*

Pray excuse me. I cannot take it.

—*Last words of President Jefferson Davis, refusing to take medicine on his deathbed, December 6, 1889*

Go back, go back and do your duty, as I have done mine, and our country will be safe. Go back, go back . . . I had rather die than be whipped.

—*A mortally wounded J. E. B. Stuart exhorting his troops to fight on without him*

He is now at rest,
and we who are left are the
ones to suffer.

—*Robert E. Lee on the death of A. P. Hill,*
Petersburg, 1865

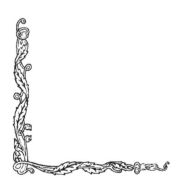

Let us pass over the river and rest under the shade of the trees.

—Stonewall Jackson's last words at the
Battle of Chancellorsville, 1863

Strike the tent!

—Robert E. Lee's final words, October 12, 1870

My religious belief teaches me to feel as safe in battle as in bed. God has fixed the time for my death. I do not concern myself about that, but to always be ready, no matter when it may overtake me.

—*Stonewall Jackson*

Well, if we are to die,
let us die like men.

—Last reported words of
Pat Cleburne, Franklin, 1864

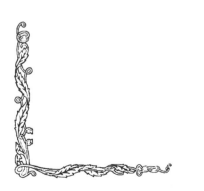

Without doing
injustice to the living,
it may safely be asserted
that our loss is irreparable; and
that among the shining hosts of the
great and good who now cluster around
the banner of the country, there exists
no purer spirit, no more heroic soul,
than that of the illustrious man
whose death I join you
in lamenting.

*—Jefferson Davis grieving the death of
General Albert Sidney Johnston, 1862*

I shall come out of this fight a live major general or a dead brigadier.

> —*Brigadier General Albert Perrin, killed in action at the Battle of Spotsylvania*

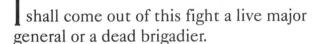

Governor Harris: General, are you wounded?

General Johnston: Yes, and I fear seriously.

> —*Last words of Albert Sidney Johnston, who bled to death at Shiloh, 1862, after being struck by a stray minié ball. A simple tourniquet could have saved his life.*

The truth is this:
The march of Providence
is so slow and our desires so
impatient; the work of progress
is so immense and our means of
aiding it so feeble; the life of humanity
is so long, that of the individual so
brief, that we often see only the
ebb of the advancing wave and
are thus discouraged. It is
history that teaches us
to hope.

—*Robert E. Lee, near the end of his life*